# spontaneous combustion

# spontaneous combustion

## combustion

setting your life on fire

*Laurel Vespi*

Library and Archives Canada Cataloguing in Publication

Vespi, Laurel, 1958-

Spontaneous combustion : setting your life on fire / Laurel
Vespi.

ISBN 978-0-9736844-3-8

1. Self-actualization (Psychology). 2. Conduct of life. I. Title.
BF637.S4V48 2008            158.1            C2008-902588-1

♾ Printed in Canada by AGMV Marquis on Rolland Opaque Natural
Edition Text acid free paper. Cover and interior design by Mieka
West

for my grandmother
who was the first person to
teach me happiness does not
depend upon circumstances

# CONTENTS

Acknowledgements ix

Foreword xi

Waiting for the #37 bus. 1

Everyone is waiting for something. 7

Why is everyone waiting? 13

    Fear 14

    Perfectionism 16

    Mediocrity 19

    Denial 21

Why set your life on fire? 25

What is spontaneous combustion? 35

Five ways to set your life on fire. 39

    Participate more and smolder less. 41

    Connect with your burning desire. 52

    Surround yourself with hot people. 66

    Figure out what fuels you. 76

    Keep stirring the fire. 86

Now what? 99

## ACKNOWLEDGEMENTS

Every creative work relies on sparks of inspiration, encouragement and genius. My deepest thanks to the following people who enrich my life and made this a work of love:

Kim Doyle Thorsen, my editor, for nitpicking, challenging me and ensuring I had clarity so my readers could have their own.

Mieka West for her artistic talents and unending patience.

Craig Kielburger for his generosity of spirit and vision.

Kim Duke, Nancy Fraser and Neela Bell, some of the hottest women I know, for never letting me settle for mediocre.

Virginia Ward for providing lifelong continuity and perspective.

Victor Vesely, my perfectly imperfect friend, for being there time after time.

Carole Rounding for her willingness to wear multiple hats; the most important of which is sister.

Emily, Hannah and Rachael for teaching me more than I will likely ever teach them.

And Frank.

For many, becoming the designer of one's own life begins with a call to action—a single moment to make a change, grab the wheel or, as Laurel Vespi would put it, set your life on fire. For me, that call to action came at the age of twelve when I discovered just how unfair the world could sometimes be, and decided to do something about it.

It was a bright morning in Toronto, Ontario, on April 19, 1995, as I woke up and got ready for another day of school. My morning ritual always included reading my favourite section of the local *Toronto Star* newspaper: the comics. As I picked up the newspaper that day, a front-page headline caught my eye: "Battled child labor, boy, 12, murdered."

The article told the story of twelve year old Iqbal Masih, a Pakistani boy who, at the age of four, was sold into child labour by his parents to repay a small family debt. After six years of working twelve hours a day chained to a carpet weaving loom, Iqbal finally managed to escape. Upon returning to his family, he quickly rose to become one of the world's youngest and most outspoken crusaders for the abolishment of child labour, traveling the world with his messages of hope and freedom. Then, in April 1995, Iqbal was shot and killed while biking in the fields around his Pakistani home. The identity of the gunman has never been determined, but he was suspected to have been a member of the local carpet mafia.

I was appalled by what I read. I sat for a moment at my kitchen table, stewing over the cruel injustices that marked Iqbal's short life and the lives of millions of other children around the world who suffered in child labour.

That was when my call to action came. I had two choices: I could hope that a change would come or I could be a part of the change. I could wait for tomorrow or I could seize *today*. I immediately tore the article out of the newspaper, stuffed it in my backpack and headed to school. When I arrived, I stood in front of my

Grade Seven classmates, read them the story and asked who among them would join me in taking action against the injustices of child labour. Eleven hands went up.

From those humble beginnings came Free The Children, the world's largest network of children helping children through education. Today, our organization works to bring education, clean water, healthcare and alternative forms of income to marginalized communities around the world and give children in need the chance for a brighter future.

Since founding Free The Children in 1995, I've had the honour of meeting some of the world's most accomplished and inspiring individuals, from Mother Teresa, to Bill Clinton, Oprah Winfrey, the Dalai Lama, Archbishop Desmond Tutu and children the world over who have faced exploitation and overcome. What binds them all together is their determination to seize today—their unwillingness to wait for tomorrow. Each of them has come to a turning point, heard their call to action and answered "yes." Each of them has set their life on fire.

On my travels around the world, speaking to audiences about social responsibility and global citizenship, I often reference the wise words of Mahatma Gandhi who once said, "You must *be the change* you wish to see in the world." You, too, can be the change. You, too, can set your life on fire. Consider *Spontaneous Combustion* your call to action, the match to light your flame.

Craig Kielburger
Free The Children
Founder and Chair

*Waiting for*
*the #37 bus.*

SITTING ON A CURB in the Piazza della Stazione, I was beginning to think that the #37 bus did not exist. My traveling companions and I had arrived in Florence from Rome by train and we were looking forward to making the relatively short journey to a beautiful country inn just outside of the city. It was hot, as July afternoons in Italy often are. And we were tired. After a day of travel, the idea of putting our feet up and enjoying a refreshing drink in the cooler Tuscan countryside was definitely appealing.

The instructions we had received seemed quite simple. Wait for the #37 bus and it will bring you directly to a stop near the inn where our hosts would collect us. So we waited at the bus stop. And we waited.

A lot of other buses came and went. A lot of people got on and off buses. No one else seemed to be waiting for the #37. After what seemed like a reasonable length of time, we telephoned our hosts. They were surprised we had not yet arrived.

"We're still waiting for the #37 bus," we explained.

"That's strange. Two #37 buses have already passed by. Are you sure you are waiting at the bus stop just outside the train station?" our hosts asked.

"Yes, we're at the bus stop just outside the train station. There's a sign that lists the #37 bus so we must be in the right place."

After a brief conversation we all agreed to wait a little longer, perhaps having missed seeing the #37 bus. Our hosts assured us that the bus should indeed be along soon. So we waited. We watched all sorts of numbered buses go by: #7, #13, #18, #23, even #36, but no #37 in sight.

Time passed. We telephoned our hosts again who reported that indeed the elusive #37 bus had come by them... again. Perhaps the combination of fatigue and heat were somehow affecting our ability to read numbers? So we waited.

More time passed. It was almost as if we had become rooted to the spot. Our lovely vision of the inn seemed to fade further and further into the distance. Eventually it seemed that quite likely we would sit on the curb in the Piazza della Stazione forever.

Until someone suggested that there had to be another way. And of course there was. We all agreed on the somewhat expensive option of hiring two taxicabs to take us to the inn.

Turned out the #37 bus actually stopped around the corner just out of sight.

Turned out the #36 bus also went where we were going.

Imagine how much more time we could have spent waiting on the curb if we hadn't finally decided to get up and look for another solution.

*Life can be just like waiting for the #37 bus.*

You can spend your whole life waiting for something that is just out of sight, while if you were only to shift slightly you would be able to see it.

You can spend your whole life waiting for something when there is another, equally perfect solution right at your fingertips.

You can spend your whole life being held back by insisting on doing something the "right" way, rather than seeing other possibilities.

You can spend your whole life sitting on the curb watching and waiting.

Or you can decide to do something different.

How much of human life
is lost in waiting!
——— *Ralph Waldo Emerson*

*Everyone is
waiting for
something.*

IT MIGHT NOT BE the #37 bus, but everyone is waiting for something. If I stood on the street corner and asked people, "What needs to happen before you start doing what you really want to do?" there would be quite the list of things they are waiting for:

- to lose weight
- to find Mr or Miss Right
- more money
- more time

- the kids to grow up
- more information
- the winning lottery ticket
- things to change
- a particular day of the week
- retirement
- somebody else to do something
- ?

*What are you waiting for?*

People seem to have an inexhaustible amount of patience when waiting for the things that are most important to them—the things that speak to their heart and soul. People dream of adventure and wait until they retire to travel, only to find that they're no longer up to the journey. They postpone taking a family photo hoping to lose twenty pounds first. Although people spend a third of their life at work, they settle for jobs they don't like. They long for a calm and peaceful existence, yet live in disorganized clutter. They take care of everyone else except themselves because they let other people's priorities take center stage. And while they say their health is important, they wait for Monday to start eating well.

People passively wait day after day, putting off decisions and actions, as if they had all the time in the world. They think, "I'll get to that when..."

The curious thing is that most people have no patience when waiting for things of little significance. They are in a hurry with all sorts of unimportant stuff like traffic jams, line-ups, microwaves or elevators. They honk their horns and stamp their feet and press that elevator button sixteen times in a futile attempt to make it come quicker. They grumble and sigh and look at their watches. They impatiently declare, "I don't have time for this."

*Are you one of those people?*

Wouldn't it be a different world if people stamped their feet and honked their horns for fulfillment and health, for dreams and relationships, for love and adventure, for peace and abundance? Wouldn't it be wonderful if people kept pressing the button for their deepest desires? Wouldn't you rather begin truly living your life now instead of someday in the future? Someday is not a day of the week. You can't find it on any calendar. What you will find is that you can end up waiting a long time for someday to arrive.

Have you ever waited outdoors in a line for something? Before the internet it was common to stand for hours and hours waiting for concert tickets, regardless of the weather. After a while your body started to stiffen. Your hands and feet got a little numb because there was not enough blood flow. Standing around waiting was a cold proposition. What did people begin to do? They started shuffling their feet and blowing on their hands. They were trying to create a little heat.

*Are you beginning to go numb*
*while waiting on your life?*

Go ahead, start shuffling your feet. Start today! You can create a spark that will let you heat up your life, and actually set it on fire.

*Are you still willing to wait for the*
*most important things in your life?*

You may delay, but time will not.
—— *Benjamin Franklin*

## Why is everyone
## waiting?

IF YOU RECOGNIZE yourself as someone who is impatient for all the wrong things, cut yourself a little slack. There are obstacles which allow people to become stuck waiting for the most important things in their lives. The most common ones are fear, perfectionism, mediocrity and denial. That list might sound ominous but these obstacles don't have to be as frightful as they sound. Recognizing which one—or ones—are true for you is the first step toward doing something about them.

## Fear

People often choose to wait on life out of fear. It's not a very good reason. Often our fears seem larger than they actually are because we have granted them such power in our lives. Fear in the face of real danger is good. Fear egged on by the little voices in your head is a poor substitute for life.

Secretly, many people are afraid they'll fail. They fear what other people will think or how they'll react. They're scared to take a risk in case it doesn't work out. They're afraid that they just don't have it in them. Some people are even afraid they'll succeed.

Fear holds us prisoner all the time. It prevents us from doing things that we are more than capable of doing and deprives us of the rewards that await us.

A few years ago while traveling in Mexico I had the opportunity to climb to the top of an ancient Mayan pyramid. It was a long way up— a long, long way. One by one my family members decided that they had reached their limit until eventually it was just me and our guide. I don't mind heights, but I'm just not comfortable with the climbing part. To be honest I was pretty afraid. To his credit the guide kept me focused on taking one step at a time until we had finally reached what I thought was the top.

I had started to congratulate myself when he said, "You have to jump onto this ledge. From there you will be able to step up onto the very top of the pyramid." To get onto that ledge I had to jump over a large gap in the stones. I told him that the spot where I was standing was accomplishment enough. I'll never forget his next words:

"You are one jump from the top of the pyramid. Are you going to let fear stop you from touching the gods?"

Saying yes would have been utterly ridiculous at that moment. So I took one deep breath, one nerve wracking leap and I got to touch the gods. It was worth it. The view from the very top was more spectacular than I imagined. Best of all, there was a real sense of sacred space. In hindsight, it was a simple thing to do, but at the time I was quite willing to settle for an "almost experience". I almost let fear hold me back. With a little encouragement and a good shot of clarity, that guide sparked me into action.

> Be not afraid of life.
> ———— *Henry James*

## Perfectionism

Sometimes people put things off because they want to get them right. They want to avoid making mistakes. They believe that with more time, energy or motivation, they will be able to do a better job. People get stuck thinking that they don't have enough information and they end up continually preparing without ever taking a step forward. They wait until they are certain they'll achieve that "picture perfect" version of whatever they're after. They really want it to be perfect.

Perfection is highly overrated—or at least misunderstood. Consider that sometimes it is the flaws in things that make them perfect. In Middle-Eastern philosophy, it's said that God is perfect so humankind doesn't need to be. That's why there is an imperfection deliberately woven into every Persian rug. In some North American native cultures, women weave flaws into their blankets. By including an irregular thread they provide a path for the soul to get out so it doesn't become stuck. In these ways of thinking, imperfection takes on a little of the divine.

Strive for excellence, not perfection. Excellence is an ongoing journey rather than a destination. It's a process of taking action, reflecting, learning and acting again. When you strive for excellence, you move along a path of continual improvement. There's no need to wait any longer because the obstacle—wanting to get it exactly right—is removed. Perfectionism is a breeding ground for waiting because in our hearts we're not sure, for whatever reason, that we can do it exactly right. How do we even know what exactly right is? Striving for excellence welcomes errors as a breeding ground for learning. If you were never meant to make mistakes, pencils wouldn't have erasers.

*Are you worried about getting everything right?*

A good garden may
have some weeds.
—— *Thomas Fuller*

## *Mediocrity*

We live in a culture of mediocrity. People seem willing to continually lower their expectations and settle for good enough. They create a life that is okay but not exceptional; adequate but not fulfilling. It might have to do with an underlying sense of unworthiness. They feel that deep down they don't deserve everything wonderful, that true happiness and contentment are not their birthright. People think that it's better to not tempt fate, particularly if things are going well. They discount the idea that the universe is an abundant place, and believe in its limits instead.

All this is not to say you shouldn't be grateful for what you have. Absolutely. Count every single blessing. But being blessed does not mean that you cannot reach for more. Consider a philosophy called shameless idealism—the idea of opening yourself up to everything that is possible without limits. When you release yourself from the constraints of what is reasonable, almost anything becomes possible. This idea was first shared with me by Canadian activists Craig and Marc Kielburger, who used their shameless idealism to develop two wonderful organizations, Free the Children and Leaders Today. Both organizations encourage young people to create positive change in the world. There isn't much room for mediocrity in the life of a shameless idealist. I was once called "ridiculously unrealistic". I took it as a compliment. When you are willing to entertain ideas that are idealistic, unrealistic, seemingly impossible, then life becomes a wonderful, rich adventure.

*What are you willing to settle for?*

## *Denial*

A lot of people believe they have all the time in the world. My grandmother lived to be ninety-nine years old. Her mother reached 102. Banking on this history of longevity, my family expected my mother to live well into her nineties. When she died of cancer at seventy-three, we were all somewhat stunned.

That's the problem with waiting. You can comfort yourself with the idea that you have time. You secretly believe that no matter how long you wait, there will still be enough time. Even though the rational part of you might say, "tomorrow is promised to no one," another part of you says "except me." Well, unless you have a crystal ball, you don't know what timeline and agenda life has in store for you.

Sometimes people wait for dramatic life-altering events to prompt change. They think a scare from the doctor will catapult them into a healthier lifestyle, or the death of someone close to them will provide the jolt required for them to enrich their relationships. You'd think that these types of events would be a catalyst for not waiting any longer. Here's a sobering statistic: 90% of patients with severe heart disease fail to change their unhealthy lifestyles, even after their doctors tell them that they're in a "change or die" situation.[1] So even when it's do or die, most people choose to keep waiting.

What's different for the other 10%? They decide they'd rather stop waiting and start re-kindling their life. They make a conscious choice. They decide that life is not to be wasted any longer. They get the big picture. They're willing to take a risk. They spontaneously combust.

*What if you have less time than you think?*

No matter what it is that has kept you waiting, right now you can choose something else. You

1  *Fast Company* Jan 2007

can decide that those obstacles are not compelling enough anymore. You can decide that the benefits of setting your life on fire far outweigh the risks.

> A ship is safe in harbor, but
> that's not what ships are for.
> —— *W.G.T. Shedd*

# *Why set your life on fire?*

WAITING IS A PRETTY comfortable place. On the surface, waiting doesn't seem to carry any risks. It certainly doesn't require much effort or energy. It doesn't have much sizzle. You don't have to change your behaviour, tackle your fears, raise the bar. Some people would argue there's a good case for waiting. It's the path of least resistance. So maybe you'd prefer to hedge your bets and play it safe. You have a lot of company if that's your current state of mind.

The problem with that comfort zone is that you begin to believe a gigantic shift is needed for something to change. That's not true. Stop waiting for a massive explosion before you begin setting your life on fire. Any change or forward motion creates friction and begins to heat things up. To start, you only need one moment of spontaneous combustion—a spark—to get things going. If you're not convinced to give up waiting and begin living a more fulfilling life, here are a couple more reasons for you to consider.

*The world is waiting for you.*

While you're hanging around waiting, the world is actually waiting for you too. Imagine the universe as a giant jigsaw puzzle. Every person holds a unique piece of the puzzle. If you've ever done a jigsaw puzzle, you know that there are all different shapes and sizes of pieces. Some might seem like they have more importance than others—like the corners or the straight edges—but in the end, the puzzle is only complete when all the pieces fit.

People are like pieces in the universal puzzle. Some people are the corners, some are the straight edges, some are the middle pieces and some are those oddly shaped ones that you can't quite figure out how they fit until suddenly it becomes obvious. And when pieces of the puzzle are missing, the picture is incomplete and everyone feels a little frustrated and certainly disappointed.

Your decision to stop waiting and to set your life on fire is a step toward contributing your piece into the universal puzzle. When you live your life fully, you have an impact on those around you. The spontaneous combustion in your life creates energy or heat that influences others to contribute their own piece. It's not important that you figure out whether you're a corner or a middle piece, or even what the big picture is, your job is just to work on your piece. When everyone contributes their own piece to the puzzle, it all eventually comes together.

And one other thing: while you keep the universe waiting, it really only has so much patience with you. If you get too comfortable in the waiting place, eventually you are going to get some uninvited assistance. First a little nudge, then a shove, then a smack on the head, then perhaps one of those dramatic life-altering events designed to really get your attention. Why wait for that?

So, if waiting is okay for you, consider this: It's not okay for the rest of us. We need you to take care of your piece.

> Our lives are connected by a
> thousand invisible threads.
> —— *Herman Melville*

*Regrets on your deathbed are tough.*

Without a doubt, you are going to die someday. Period. End of story. Don't think of that in a depressing way. Think of it as a call to action. Life has a best-before date, but you just can't quite read the label. You can make a conscious choice to stop waiting and start living fully today. If you don't, and you spend your life fearful, too comfortable, or in denial, you are going to be sorry. Guaranteed.

Can you imagine anyone on their final day in this life saying the following? "You know, I wasted a lot of time and opportunities. I never really did or said the things I wanted to. I let things slip through my fingers. But it's okay. I have no regrets about it." No, it's more likely a person would say, "If only I had a little more time. If only I had taken a chance. If only I had not been so afraid." It's likely that you will regret most the things you did not do, rather than the things you did.

*If only....*

Regret is an insight that comes a day too late. Save yourself the disappointment that will come later in life. Give up waiting today. Instead choose now to spark the fire in your life. At the end of your days be able to say, "I lived well. My life burned brightly."

> One's real life is often the life
> that one does not lead.
> —— *Oscar Wilde*

*One more consideration.*

There's an old saying that good things come to those who wait. On the surface that sounds like pretty good motivation for holding off. Perhaps that saying should be: good things come to those who are patient. There's a fundamental difference between waiting and patience. When you wait, you are counting on something external to get the ball rolling. Waiting is a passive activity—like sitting on a curb in Italy.

Patience, on the other hand, occurs after planning and action. It's a state of mind that trusts that once you have initiated action, results will begin to appear. You simply might have to be patient. Not everything you want will happen at once. Some things take time and hard work. Waiting is an excuse for your inaction. Patience creates the space for your actions to take effect.

> One cannot reap immediately
> where one has sown.
> —— *Søren Kierkegaard*

There's a proverb that captures the idea of patience perfectly: "Pray to God and row for the shore." You could wait for someone else to take charge, even wait for divine intervention. You might be waiting for a long, long time. Or you can take responsibility to make things happen. Pray, *and* if there is something that *you* can be doing that moves you forward, then do it. Take whatever action you can and trust that things will fall into place to support you.

> Patience is the companion
> of wisdom.
> —— *Saint Augustine*

So, you could wait for a bolt of lightning to ignite you. The problem with that strategy is, in the big scheme of things, it doesn't happen all that often. Your chances of being hit by lightning are only about 1 in 600,000. Not great odds. Why not decide to create your own spark instead?

*Are you ready to stop waiting?*

*Is it time for a little spontaneous combustion?*

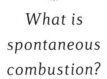

# What is
# spontaneous
# combustion?

SPONTANEOUS COMBUSTION occurs in each moment you decide to take action. Remember the #37 bus? When we finally decided that we were not going to sit on the curb any longer, that we were going to look for another solution, that was the moment something different started to happen. It is the moment of decision when all things become possible.

I understand how tempting it is to avoid the decision. I'm not really a willing early morning exerciser. The appeal of that warm and cozy bed is just too great. I know all of the reasons why it's the best time of the day to put in a workout, particularly for me, but some days I can come up with some really convincing counter-arguments. Lying there having the "will I or won't I" debate with myself is just another form of waiting.

When Nike created their "Just Do It" campaign they knew what they were talking about. A lot of time and opportunity passes by when you wait. For all of us, when we decide to get up and our feet hit the floor, we have turned intention into action. That's when the fire is sparked.

If you have been busy waiting, putting your life on hold for that elusive someday, it's time for a little combustion. You have the match in your hands. Just light the fire. Once you do, everything becomes a little easier.

It's easier to keep a fire burning than to start one from scratch.

It's easier to ignite one part of your life when you have another part sizzling.

Spontaneous combustion is not a one-time event. It's the repeated commitment to action;

the ongoing desire to keep the fire burning; each in-the-moment decision to move forward. It's the willingness to translate good intentions into great actions. It's the spark that lets everything become possible.

*Five ways to set
your life on fire.*

ONCE YOU'VE SPONTANEOUSLY combusted—made the decision that you are no longer content with waiting—you've created a spark from which you can truly set your life on fire. Now that you've committed to the idea of living a life on fire, here are some practical strategies that will help to fan the flames:

- Participate more and smolder less.
- Connect with your burning desire.
- Surround yourself with hot people.
- Figure out what fuels you.
- Keep stirring the fire.

You don't need to jump into all five at once, unless you want to. Feeling like you must take it all on is just part of the perfectionism game. Choose one that is a good fit for you right now and begin there. Once you've got that underway, go back to the list and choose again.

*Participate more and smolder less.*

Have you ever sat mesmerized in front of a fire? The changing colours, the dancing flames, the snapping and popping wood draws you in and holds your attention. You keep staring and don't even notice how much time has gone by. You've become a passive observer. Sure, you can feel the heat from the fire and it's nice and cozy sitting there, but nothing is really required of you. When you're busy watching and waiting, your own fire smolders rather than ignites.

In North America we live in a culture that encourages us to watch rather than participate in life. That's part of the appeal of reality television. We can live vicariously through other people, all from the comfort of a recliner chair. It might satisfy some desire as entertainment but it is a poor substitute for creating one's own reality.

We shy away from rich conversations because we want to be politically correct. We let our inner critics list the 101 reasons why we

41

shouldn't take a risk. We come up with excuses for why we can't do something—not enough time, not enough money, not enough information. We trade active participation in life for simply watching. And then what happens? People who long to see the world spend their time watching travel shows instead of hopping on a plane, people who desire deep connection have mundane conversations rather than thought-provoking ones, and people who want more settle for less.

I'm not suggesting that observing life should be avoided. Observation can provide you with new insights, valuable information and inspiration. The problem with watching is that it can consume a lot of time. Pay attention to how much time you spend watching rather than participating. When you live life primarily as an observer, you pass up opportunities to fan the flames of your own fire. You become passive and inactive. You watch rather than do; smolder rather than ignite.

Smoldering fires need oxygen. Breathe some life into yours by trying one of these ideas:

∷ *Embrace today as the greatest day.*
There's a saying, "Tomorrow is the busiest day of the week." That's because so many people put off what they could do today until tomorrow. We've all heard the phrase *carpe diem.* Of course the "seize the day" philosophy is connected to the idea that we never know how many tomorrows we have. True enough.

There's another reason to embrace today as the greatest day. You want to make the most of the opportunities that are in front of you today. They may not come your way again. The universe is continually providing you with opportunities for you to move closer to what you want. Sometimes the message is crystal clear. Other times these opportunities are a little more ambiguous. And sometimes you miss them because they look like challenges or hard work.

Today is the greatest day because it holds unique possibilities. Start your day by asking yourself these questions:

*How will I participate in life today?*

*What unique opportunities are here today for the taking?*

Seize one of them.

> We cannot waste time. We
> can only waste ourselves.
> —— *George M. Adams*

∴ *Give less energy to worrying.*
Sometimes people choose to watch rather than participate in life because they are concerned

about what might happen. They're afraid things might not turn out how they expect so they hedge their bets and do nothing. They play the what-if game, which is always a losing proposition. Worrying allows you to remain passive.

The truth about worrying is that it is the most unproductive use of your time. The act of worrying never changed anything. It's both reassuring and sobering to know that the vast majority of things that you worry about never come to pass. Of the small percentage of things you worry about that do happen, most are completely out of your control. There's not a darn thing that you could have done to change them. Of the things that keep you awake at night, there are only a very few that you could have acted on to possibly change the outcome. Ironically, even in those instances, you likely choose worry over planning and action.

Shantideva, an eighth-century Buddhist monk asked,

*If you can solve your problem then what is the need of worrying?*

*If you cannot solve it, then what is the use of worrying?*

That's a pretty great perspective. When you find yourself stuck worrying, take the monk's advice. Ask yourself:

> *Is there something I can do to make this situation different?*

If the answer is yes, then go for it. If the answer is no, then take a deep breath, and put the energy you're using worrying to better use.

> I have been through some
> terrible things in my life, some
> of which actually happened.
> —— *Mark Twain*

⁞ *Let observation act as kindling.*

There's much to be learned from watching. It's often observation that creates awareness—you begin to see the world or yourself differently. You notice things that you might not have noticed before. While observation can be a great catalyst, too often we don't take advantage of the spark it could ignite. We gain some new insight but don't act on it, momentarily get excited but let the moment pass, think "that would be cool" but give in to excuses.

Don't let this happen. When you do engage in observation, use it as kindling to light your fire. There are opportunities all around you to turn what might simply be passive activities into fire starting action. Let's say you read a great book or watch an interesting movie. Rather than letting the ideas presented smolder inside you, fan your flame by using it as a springboard for a rich conversation with someone. When you have a little "aha" moment, seize it and ask yourself:

*What does this mean in my life?*

It's good to step back and observe but the key is to then do something with the new information you have. Go ahead and watch, then participate.

:: *Challenge yourself.*

Jot down all of the things you want to do, try or learn. Think of it as your lifelong to-do list. The idea of creating such a list is not a new one. John Goddard is often credited for the popularity of the "life goals" concept. When he was fifteen years old, Goddard wrote a list of 127 things that he wanted to accomplish in his life. It included everything from learning to fence to climbing Mt. Kilimanjaro; from riding an elephant to visiting the Eiffel Tower. Now in his seventies, Goddard has checked off 109 items on his life list, at last count. You can bet that John Goddard has lived an interesting and fulfilling life. You can also bet that he isn't a guy that believes in watching rather than participating.

A life list gives you a structure for planning and decision-making. It helps to maintain a focus on the kind of life you want to live. Don't worry too much about *how* you will do all of the things on your list. It's more important to capture *what* experiences you want to have. Once you begin to focus on making something happen, the details in many cases will begin to take care of themselves. It's a combination of focus and faith. Begin making your life-list today.

> Only those who will risk going
> too far can possibly find
> out how far one can go.
> —— *T.S. Eliot*

∴ *Give up mediocre.*

It's ironic. In the things that are most important to us, often we ask very little of ourselves. We cut corners and lower our standards. We compromise our values so they fit the path of least resistance. We say one thing but we do another and as a result our actions are not always a good reflection of the things that matter most to us. Sometimes, as the saying goes, we just phone it in.

Why does that happen? It could be that your days are filled to overflowing with activities that do not necessarily reflect your priorities. It could be that you have been seduced by the cultural value of quantity rather than quality. It could be that you have gotten used to doing more rather than doing better. In the face of such obstacles, it seems easier to settle for mediocre.

You probably feel like you don't have the time and energy to do more in your life. Giving up mediocre is not about doing more things, it's about doing things differently. It's about doing less and doing it well. Giving up mediocre is about saying, "X, Y and Z are no longer nego-tiable for me." Do it. Give up mediocre. Decide where to set your personal bar on the things that matter most to you. Chances are, in certain areas of your life, you let things slide. You are the best judge of where you need to focus. This process is not about perfection. Repeat—it's not about perfection or things never being good enough. It's about excellence; holding yourself to a par-ticular standard and making choices daily that reflect what matters to you most.

Full participation in life lets you end your day with a feeling of contentment and satisfac-tion. If all you ever give is half an effort, all you will see are half the results. There's a great line in the movie *Thelma and Louise*: "You get the life you settle for." Go ahead and set the bar high.

> We are what we repeatedly do.
> Excellence then is not
> an act but a habit.
> —— *Aristotle*

*Connect with your burning desire.*

We all have a desire to have meaning in our lives, to feel that we are making a contribution, that in some way our time on this planet counts for something. Figuring out our purpose though can feel a bit like trying to light a soggy log—lots of smoke and not much fire. Our days get so busy that finding clarity about our life purpose ends up shuffled down to the bottom of our to-do list. When we don't have a sense of why we are here and the difference we can make, life feels more like drudgery than bliss.

The mere idea of "life purpose" can be overwhelming for some people. But if you keep in mind a few basics about purpose, you may feel more ready to uncover your burning desire. First, there is no dream too big. If you can conceive it, you can achieve it. You might not know how, but if you can articulate your dream, then you can discover a way to make it happen. Next, the combination of focus plus passion creates change. When you figure out what you are

52

passionate about and direct your energy toward it, change inevitably occurs. And lastly, purpose is not just a "nice to have" concept. It's a "need to have" element. Purpose serves as the principle around which you can organize your life. It lights the way and gives you a framework for making choices.

Beginning to connect with your burning desire is not as difficult as you might think. Try these ideas:

:: *Do some personal work.*

It's not uncommon for people have a low level of self-awareness because they simply don't take the time for personal reflection. Between loads of laundry there doesn't seem to be any room for exploring thoughts, feelings and attitudes, except in the most superficial sense. Getting to know yourself can be a fascinating journey— indeed it is a lifelong journey. There are great questions to explore, such as:

What are my personal strengths and
    weaknesses?
What are my core values?
What impact do I have on others?
What is not negotiable for me?
What is my biggest blind spot?

These are just some examples of the powerful questions that can lead you to new insights, areas of personal growth, clarity and self respect.

*How well do you know yourself?*

Dedicate some time for your own personal growth. Ask yourself the big questions. Figure out where you stand on issues. Confront yourself more. Read thought-provoking books. Keep a journal. Engage in rich conversations.

> Our truest life is when we
> are in dreams awake.
> —— *H. D. Thoreau*

:: *Go ahead even if you are stuck.*

If you are feeling stuck, there's a tendency to stay stuck. You might be thinking, "I have no idea what my life purpose is so I won't do anything different until I have a revelation!" Feeling stuck is just another kind of waiting. You could wait your whole lifetime for all the pieces of your burning desire to fall into place. And you are not tied to it once you begin, what feels like your purpose at one point in your life may not be what lights you on fire at a later time. Being stuck sometimes is really about feeling a need to have it all figured out. Cut yourself some slack and decide to not worry about it so much.

You don't have to get overwhelmed by life purpose if you are feeling like you can't figure it out. Take a simple step toward your burning desire. Ask yourself:

*What's the one thing I stand for?*

Choose a principle that really resonates with you—perhaps love or joy or simplicity. Then become the poster child for that quality. Become the living embodiment of it. As you go about your day, look for opportunities to practice that quality. It's not about doing it perfectly. It's about bringing more of it into the world. Don't feel that you have to stay with any one quality you choose. Change when it feels right. You can even pick a "quality of the day," something that you will take a stand for that day. Then choose again the next day.

Some time ago, I chose to stand for compassion. It's a great way for me to shift my focus away from judgment—to see other people's situations and be able to support or encourage them.

Compassion is an act of loving-kindness. It taps into a desire for inner and outer peace. When I find myself compassionately challenged, I try to ask myself, "What is the most generous explanation for this?" It helps to point me in a different direction.

> Life is a promise: fulfill it.
> ――― *Mother Teresa*

∴ *Write your obituary.*

Open any newspaper to the obituary section and you will get a glimpse into people's lives.

He was loved and enjoyed by all who met him.

She will be remembered for her sense of humour, commitment to family and friends and her love of conversation.

He was a kind and warm man with a friendly and quiet manner.

She will be remembered for her kindness and generosity of spirit.

*What is it you want people to be saying about you when you are no longer here?*

The greatest legacy you leave behind won't be a donation of a large sum of money to some worthy cause. When you read obituaries of philanthropists, it becomes apparent that their personal qualities had the most impact on other people, not their chequebooks. Your true legacy is created each day in the smallest actions. They define your life. Once you are gone, no one will say you were generous of spirit if that's not how you lived your life day to day. Simple, consistent gestures truly reflect who you are. Whether it's with your family, friends, coworkers or strangers, how you choose to show up in the world has the power to encourage, influence and inspire.

Sit down and write your obituary. Think about how you would like to be remembered. Now each day let your words and deeds be a conscious reflection of that burning desire.

> Act as if what you do makes
> a difference. It does.
> —— *William James*

:: *Become a socially-conscious global citizen.*
I used to think that it was enough to focus on performing small acts to make a difference in the world. Random acts of kindness that have the power to impact those around us in amazing ways, sometimes in ways we never realize. I'm still a believer in the capacity for small gestures to create huge change. I just don't think it's sufficient anymore.

It's time to look at our contributions outside of ourselves and our families. We need to begin to think globally. People often shy away from that idea because they just can't quite figure out how to do it, or because the world's problems seem so big or because they think one person can't make a difference.

It's time to become engaged in a global discussion—about the environment, poverty, human rights, intolerance, inequality, disease and hunger. Global problems require a global response. They are no longer isolated to some obscure part of the world that you have never heard of. These problems exist in some form in your own community. It's not enough any longer to say "I'm too busy," or "That doesn't really apply to me." It's time to participate in the most significant conversations of our lifetime. Not only do you have gifts and talents to share, there is much for you to learn from our global neighbours.

*Where to begin?*

Pay attention to what is going on in the world. Given the horror or magnitude of some global situations, it's tempting to tune out the details. Become more informed. You'll begin to see some of the ways issues are, or could be, addressed. You'll be better able to recognize how what's going on in the world is reflected in your own backyard.

Take the leap and participate in an international development project in another country. There are many fine organizations you can volunteer with for as little as two weeks. Perhaps that would be a great way to use your vacation time.

Do you need to travel to a developing country? No, not necessarily. Closer to home there are also organizations that address global issues at a local level—homeless shelters, food banks, women's shelters and lunch programs, for example. Find one that speaks to you and donate your time. It's becoming more popular for companies to allow employees paid time off for volunteer activities. If your company is not one of them, begin that conversation.

Look for opportunities to support projects you believe in. These are some of the organizations that really resonate with me. *Kiva* is a non-profit organization that facilitates micro-financing to individuals in developing countries. For as little as $25 you can loan money to someone who is building a business with the intent to break out of the poverty cycle. *Leaders Today* offers a youth leadership program that helps to create social change-makers through training and volunteer projects. Its sister organization *Free the Children*, has an Adopt a Village program which supports community development for marginalized children and their families. Do some research of your own. Find a project that you believe in and become involved. There is no shortage of ways to become a more socially-conscious global citizen. It just requires you to have hope and a desire to take action.

Never doubt that a small group
of committed people can
change the world; indeed, it is
the only thing that ever has.
—— *Margaret Mead*

*∷ Decide what you want to be*
*when you grow up.*

One of the confusions I often hear from people,
particularly in mid-life is, "I don't know what
I want to be when I grow up." So many people
come to a point in their lives when they realize
that they have a sense of dissatisfaction about
the work they do. Sometimes it's because they
never really loved their job and now they have
less tolerance for it. Sometimes they have just
outgrown it and it's no longer a good fit for their
strengths and interests. And sometimes people
reach a point when they begin looking for more
meaning or fulfillment in their lives.

Feeling that urge to discover what you want to be when you grow up is just a reflection of your burning desire. Consider what you would do if time, money and experience didn't limit you. Think back to when you were younger. What did you want to be then? What about that was appealing to you? Perhaps there is a new career path for you to choose.

Here's another thought. Notice that the question is always what do I want to *be*, not what do I want to *do*. It's great when your work is a good reflection of your burning desire. But that isn't always the case. Changing careers may not be a practical option. Ask yourself:

*How do I want to be?*

Make a list of what you want more of and what you want less of in your life. Your burning desire may be more closely related to the way you live your life than what you do for a living.

Let the beauty you love
be what you do.
—— *Rumi*

*Surround yourself with hot people.*

Modern philosopher Jim Rohn says that you are the average of the five people you spend the most time with. Stop and think about those five people in your life.

> Who are they?
> Do they support and encourage you?
> Do they provide a spark of inspiration
>     when you need it?
> Or do they overtly or subtly sabotage
>     you?

There are three kinds of people you encounter in life. Each type radiates a different kind of energy. Every person you interact with is either hot, warm or cold. The cold people in your life are probably pretty easy to identify. They are negative, cynical and critical. They tell you right to your face why you are wrong, unrealistic or crazy. They have a mantra of "you can't," and they live in the land of waiting. When you spend time with them, they do whatever they can to douse your fire. Cold people often travel in packs because misery loves miserable company. Where you find one cold person, you're likely to find more: staff lunch rooms in toxic workplaces, dinner tables of dysfunctional families or many talk radio shows. Negative thinking depletes endorphins, those feel-good chemicals in your brain, and leads to more negative thinking. Cold people help to perpetuate a nasty cycle of discouragement and gloom.

Warm people are a little trickier to figure out. Some of them are just cruising in the neutral zone. They are not really anyone's champion or supporter. They don't get too excited about anything. Fire and passion are not high on their list.

Some warm people look hot on the surface. But really, deep down they're pretty frosty. They talk the good talk, but don't walk the walk very well. They say they want you to succeed, but subtly undermine your efforts and confidence. They might talk about you in unsupportive ways behind your back.

Warm people have a narrow "me-first" view. They filter your dreams through a lens of "What does it mean to me?" They are only supportive of, or comfortable with, your success if it won't have an impact on them. Think of warm people as wet blankets that quietly smother fires. Why? Perhaps they feel threatened in some way—that your success makes them feel smaller by comparison. Mostly, no matter what they say on the outside, on the inside they're afraid of life. Their fears and limiting beliefs spill over into what they think is practical or realistic for you.

Hot people want for you what you want. They ask questions like "How can I help?" "What do you need?" Their thoughts and actions are designed to support you. They lift you up, they inspire and challenge you. They leave you feeling like you absolutely can and will achieve success. They share strategies, keep you accountable, help you get unstuck and keep you moving forward.

Not all hot people have to be physically involved in your life. Hot people can support you from a distance in some ways. In fact, you don't even have to know someone for them to create heat in your life. Being inspired by a role model, living or dead, can have just as big an impact. Hot people understand the connectivity of life—that we are all linked together in one giant energy field—and that when your life's on fire, it sets off a chain reaction for other people's lives. Hot people have the big picture in mind.

Fires don't burn well if they are in a tightly closed space or smothered. The warm and cold people in your life don't give you much room to breathe, let alone ignite. So it's critical that you begin to surround yourself with the people who light you on fire.

Feeling bad for those cold and warm people? Not to worry. We don't all share the same hot people. Someone who is warm or cold for you might just be sizzling for somebody else. Who's hot for you?

Try these ideas:

∴ *Hot people are represented in hot ideas.*
Take a close look at the books and magazines you read and the movies and television you watch. Quite simply, you are a reflection of the ideas you surround yourself with. Garbage in—garbage out. That's not to say that you have to cleanse your life completely of brainless television or fluffy movies. I know I like to read what I call "beach books" as a way to relax sometimes. It's the volume of junk that you consume that dampens your fire. Take inventory of how much time you give away to junk. Try the 80/20 rule; 80% of the time choose wisely and 20% of the time don't worry so much about the intrinsic value of what you are watching or reading. It works just like junk food for your body—one cookie never got anyone into trouble, it's the whole bag that will do you in. Look for books and media that challenge you, introduce new ideas, inspire you and form the basis for great conversation.

One's mind, once stretched
by a new idea, never regains
its original dimensions.
———— *Oliver Wendell Holmes*

∴ *Follow the leader.*

People who have already done what you want to do can be really hot for you. Finding a mentor or hiring an expert can go a long way in providing support and strategies that work. It's not that you can't find your own way. It's just that learning from the leaders can sometimes fast-track things or save you from re-inventing the wheel. You don't necessarily need to connect with someone personally. Discover who has gone before you, study what and how they did it, and then use that wisdom to your advantage.

∷ *Partner with a coach.*

A life coach's role is to support you on your journey to the successful attainment of your goals. Having a coach is like having a strategist, cheerleader and sounding board all in one. More and more people are discovering that partnering with a life coach is a great way to find clarity, overcome obstacles, increase confidence and design a plan for having what they want. Many of my clients are simply stuck for some reason and together we create fresh perspectives, new strategies and forward momentum. They begin to see that what once seemed out of reach or impossible is completely attainable. A life coach will be one of the hottest people in your life.

∷ *Clean your emotional house.*

Somewhere along the way it became an acceptable idea that once someone is in our life, they are there to stay. For some of our relationships that's true, such as a life-long partner or our dearest friend or great aunt Edna. It's also true that relationships change. If they didn't, life would be pretty stagnant. Sometimes we realize that we have a relationship that is not particularly healthy. Sometimes what was once a great friendship isn't any longer. People grow apart and no longer share the same perspectives or goals.

Just like your closets or basement, your emotional space needs decluttering every now and then. You only have so much time and energy so it's important to make conscious choices about which relationships you give your attention to. Begin to distance yourself from your cold and warm relationships so that there is more room for hot ones. Is this a difficult task? Depends on the relationship. With some people it's easy to reduce the amount of time you spend with them. Creating new boundaries and expectations can sometimes be more challenging with family members. A good way to start is to just be more aware of all of your relationships, with acquaintances, colleagues, friends and relatives, and consider how willing you are to trade your time for their negative energy.

:: *Build a success circle of hot people.*
It really is all about making conscious choices about who you will spend your time with. Take notice of who "gets you"—the people who see you for who you are and appreciate you because of it. Those people will want to support you. There are likely people in your life right now that fit the bill. Consciously create your own success circle—a group of people who are like your own personal board of advisors. Ask them if they will be on call to provide guidance and support. Perhaps set up a regular meeting time during which you can brainstorm ideas and solutions. This may feel like a stretch if you are not comfortable asking others for help. Be clear about what you want or need from your success circle, take a deep breath and just ask. You'll be surprised at how willing hot people are to lend a hand.

Become a heat-seeking missile. You know when you are in the presence of a hot person. Spend more time with them. Look for other people, perhaps even ones that you don't know yet, who share a similar goal or philosophy. Find out where they hang out and go there. Join a club. Be hot for someone else—when you reach out to support others, you'll find your temperature goes up. The hottest people I know are surrounded by other sizzling people.

> We deceive ourselves when we fancy that only weakness needs support. Strength needs it far more.
> ——— *Madame Anne Sophie Swetchine*

*Figure out what fuels you.*

In order for a fire to keep burning, it needs fuel. After that initial combustion, a fire needs a steady and continual supply of fuel and oxygen. Without these elements, a fire eventually dies down and becomes a pile of ash. That's why it's so important to figure out what sustains your fire. Sometimes people think that they can let their fire dwindle and just put in one big effort to restart the blaze. The truth is it's difficult to light a log with a match. You need to "step up" a fire—consistently add little bits of fuel to keep the fire going—not just one big surge every now and then.

When you feel fueled, it seems so much easier to go after your dreams, keep your priorities in line, withstand distractions and overcome obstacles. Think of the last time you allowed yourself to run on empty for a while. Chances are you did not feel energetic, inspired or capable. You likely switched into survival mode—which is just another form of waiting. Refueling every

once in a while is not enough. You need to consistently restore yourself.

Once a fire is well established it has a super-
hot core, and then it's easier to keep it burning.
Try these ideas to keep yourself fueled:

∷ *Just breathe.*

A fire does not burn without oxygen. People
do not live without air. The breath is the most
basic element of life. It's so simple, yet most of us
take it for granted until we catch a cold or find
ourselves in a smoky room. It's no surprise that
breath shows up in many common expressions
that are about slowing down or appreciating
something: catch your breath; take a breath;
breathe it in; breathtaking. Conscious breathing
is even used for pain management in childbirth.
At any time, you can elicit a relaxation response
in your body just by breathing deeply. Use your
breath to calm and center yourself.

The breath is the best place to begin when
you need refueling. The word *spirit* comes from

the Latin *spiritus*, meaning breath. Think of the act of conscious breathing as a way to reconnect with your spirit. Become more aware of your breathing. Do you tend to take shallow breaths? Most people breathe in their upper chest, using only a small portion of their lung capacity. Make it a habit to stop periodically throughout your day and take a few deep breaths. It will allow you to become fully present in the moment and reconnect with your body. Use your breathing as a way to calm yourself. When you find you are becoming stressed, anxious or overwhelmed, stop and breathe.

> Smile, breathe and go slowly.
> —— *Thich Nhat Hanh*

∷ *Find a place.*
For me, it's the ocean. I always feel re-energized when I am near the water. There something

about the sound of the waves and the rhythmic pattern of the tide that makes me feel more connected to myself and the world. Whenever I have the chance, I escape to our beach house on Vancouver Island. It's a place to relax and reflect. Whether I'm there alone or with my family, time at the beach always refuels me.

*Where do you feel most restored?*

Most people's first answer is their own home. That's great—it's wonderful to feel that your home is a sanctuary. Create a special corner in your home that is just for you. Surround yourself with things or images of things that you love and that feed your soul.

Consider where else you feel refueled. There's likely an aspect of nature that speaks to you. Maybe it's mountains, water, forest, open spaces. Make a conscious effort to discover a place that resonates with you and begin to spend time there.

It's also important to be able to connect with your special place even when you are not physically there. I can't get to the beach nearly as often as I'd like. But I have a collection of flat stones from our beach throughout our house. I only have to hold one in my hand to transport myself back there. Find a memento or a photo that takes you back to your special place.

∴ *Create a daily ritual.*

A ritual is something that you do regularly and consistently. It's a practice that restores and reconnects you. It serves to bring you back to what is important and honours a commitment to taking time just for you.

Your particular rituals will be unique to you. What refuels one person does not necessarily work for another. Experiment to find the right fit for you. Author Christina Baldwin begins her day with a prayer which contains a list of intentions—she calls them her "seven whispers of spiritual common sense". Think of Baldwin's list as guiding principles for her life. Some are: "maintain peace of mind" and "surrender to surprise". The act of reciting them each morning as a daily ritual serves to reaffirm her intentions.

> *What would be on your list*
> *of guiding principles?*

It's very important that you perform your ritual on a daily basis. It's not something that you slide into your day if there is enough time or energy left over. You need to make a personal commitment to restoring yourself and reconnecting to what is most important to you.

Here are some other ideas for a daily ritual:

keep a journal
meditate
take a walk

stretch or do yoga
read inspirational material
practice silence

∷ *Honour your body.*

Think of your body as a temple. It's the tempo-rary home on earth for your soul—the place where your spirit has sanctuary. Sadly, many of our temples are looking more like some kind of ancient ruin. Caring for your physical self is a way to restore your spiritual self. It's the ulti-mate act of respect.

*What image do you hold of your body?*

When we look at ancient ruins, we imag-ine them in all their former glory. Few people go to the Acropolis and say well that's a pile of rubble. Do you have negative thoughts or make disparaging comments about your body parts?

No matter the current state of your physical self, you can begin today to see the temple of your body with that same vision. It's not about "six pack abs" or fitting into a size 2. It's about having gratitude and respect for the body you have. Every day your body gives you the best that it can, and that best is a reflection of how well you are caring for it. So think kindly of your body and then begin choosing new or different ways to restore it.

There are some simple things you can do to honour your body. And yes, you already know them. Feed yourself well, get adequate rest, exercise and reduce stress. Knowing what to do is not sufficient. You actually have to do it. Shift your thinking. Know that every time you choose something that honours your physical self, you are paying respect to your spiritual self.

The body is a sacred garment.
—— *Martha Graham*

∴ *Use sound.*

Sound has the amazing ability to create physical, emotional, mental and spiritual balance in the body. It invites us to connect with ourselves, one another and the universe. Sound can come from many sources: music, voice, nature or silence.

*What role does sound play in your life?*

Many people are accustomed to sound in the form of background noise. They turn on the radio or TV but don't really listen to it. Consciously invite sound into your life as a way to refuel. Find music that creates energy in your body. Play that music when you need a boost. Discover music that soothes you or brings you to tears. For me one of the most spiritually moving pieces of music is "Om Namo Bhagavate" by Deva Premal. The first time I heard it was during the relaxation segment of a yoga class. It seemed like it was somehow singing my spirit. Whenever I listen to it, I feel a sense of deep connection. Experiment with the full range of music available to you.

Using your voice can also be a way to refuel. Chanting, which is simply singing prayer or vocal meditation, has been a form of spiritual restoration for centuries. And, on the other hand, do not underestimate the power of silence—the absence of sound—as a restorative tool. It is often in silence that you can hear the things that the usual noise of the day drowns out. When you can quiet your mind, you are more able to hear the sound of your spirit speaking within you.

> Let us be silent, that we may
> hear the whispers of the gods.
> ―― *Ralph Waldo Emerson*

*Keep stirring the fire.*

Every fire needs a poke every now and then. You have to shift things around to keep the fire burning. Once you do that, new wood is exposed, more oxygen becomes available and suddenly different flames pop up. The fire burns better.

You have to poke your life every once in a while too. Maintaining the status quo or approaching life in a "same-old-same-old" fashion is a sure way to dampen your fire. You need new ideas, new challenges and new ways of thinking in order to keep things burning well.

Some of the most wonderful moments with my coaching clients are when they say, "I've never thought of it that way before." Seeing something differently is the first step toward doing something differently. As soon as you shift from one spot to another, even just a slightly different one, then all kinds of things that weren't possible before, now are.

Try this: Stand with your nose pressed up against the wall. What can you see? Probably not much. Take two giant steps backwards. What can you see now? Certainly more than you could before. Turn around 180 degrees. Now what can you see? All of a sudden you see things that weren't anywhere in your field of vision before.

Most of the time we are standing with our noses pressed up against the wall. We have a very narrow focus on life. We get stuck looking at the world with the same ideas, habits, attitudes and beliefs. It's easy for the fire to go out then.

> Change your thoughts and
> you change your world.
> —— *Norman Vincent Peale*

Try these ideas:

∴ *Shift your attitude.*

You'll know it's time for a shift in attitude if you catch yourself saying, "Well, that's just the way it is." Or when you feel like you have no options, that you are stuck or if life seems like more work than play. Sometimes you might need a shift in attitude in only one area—things are cooking on all the burners but one. And sometimes you need a radical shift.

Ask yourself:

> *What are all the other ways*
> *I could think about this?*

Even if some of them seem like a stretch, just the act of brainstorming a new list of perspectives helps you to see that indeed there are other ways to think about something. And if there are other ways, then challenge yourself to choose one that feels more empowering and less stuck. If you need help, ask someone in your success circle.

Make a commitment to stop whining. It's easy to complain about life without ever doing anything to change it. Sure, we all need to let off a little steam every once in a while. It's okay to be able to unload the things that are pushing our buttons or to indulge in a pity party. But there's a difference between venting and whining. If you spend more than five minutes detailing the unfairness of it all before you move on, then you're just whining. Go ahead and vent. Tell your sad tale and then decide what you want to do about it.

Here's another attitude to consider. You are as happy in your life right now as you have made up your mind to be. That idea gets a strong reaction from some people. Usually it's because they have gotten the state of happiness confused with a certain set of events or circumstances. They think, "I'll be happy when..."

Here's the shift: happiness is not dependent on circumstances—not money, not merchandise, not even health. When you finally embrace that concept and make it work in your life, simply amazing things begin to happen. The most important thing is that you stop waiting.

If you want to be happy, be.
—— *Leo Tolstoy*

∷ *Shift your energy level.*
Remember your basic physics: a body at rest tends to stay at rest; a body in motion tends to stay in motion. That's the definition of inertia.

*Are you experiencing some kind of inertia in your life?*

You might be waiting to take some action. You might feel stuck and unable to move forward. You might be overwhelmed by how and where to start. If that's the case, it's going to take some kind of effort to get you going. Not necessarily an enormous effort, just something to get you in motion.

The trick to overcoming inertia is to just do something. Do one thing differently and you will begin to create some motion. If you want to eat better, you might begin with simply substituting one thing you eat rather than overhauling your whole diet. If you live in a state of clutter, it might begin with cleaning out one closet rather than taking on the whole house. Don't underestimate the power of a little movement to create forward momentum.

> When there is a start to
> be made, don't step over!
> Start where you are.
> ——— *Edgar Cayce*

∷ *Shift your focus.*

Whatever you focus on tends to increase. If you focus on what you don't have, you'll find that you have a greater sense of scarcity in your life. Alternately, if you focus on what you already have, you'll likely experience a greater sense of abundance. Shifting your focus, even for a short while, is a great way to stir the fire.

Some years ago I was running in the Venice Marathon in Italy. It wasn't my first marathon and I was looking forward to celebrating another fine race at the finish line. It was going great until I came to the almost inevitable point in any marathon—when everything gets really hard. Everyone seemed to be passing me. I was tired. My legs felt dead. I couldn't quite find my rhythm. I was getting a little cranky. And then seemingly out of nowhere, a runner fell into step beside me.

"How's it going?" he asked. So I told him. I began listing off a litany of complaints. He listened, and when I paused to take a breath, he asked, "How's your left arm?"

92

My left arm? I looked at him like he was crazy. Apparently he hadn't been listening all that well. "My left arm is fine," I said. "It's my legs and my back and my feet."

"Well then," he said, "Focus on your left arm." He smiled and picked up his pace and left me with that piece of advice.

As I watched him disappear into the crowd, his suggestion distracted me from my complaints. Just that simple shift in focus made the next few miles easier.

*What are you focusing on?*

If it keeps your fire stoked, great. If not, make a shift and focus on something different.

> What we see depends mainly
> on what we look for.
> —— *Sir John Lubbock*

∴ *Shift to synchronicity.*

Consider that the universe wants you to succeed. It wants you to set your life on fire and keep it burning. Remember you're a part of the giant puzzle. In essence, the universe is collaborating with you. It sends you little signs that you are on the right path. This is called synchronicity—seemingly inexplicable, almost magical events in which everything seems to line up in just the right way. We often dismiss synchronicity as luck or coincidence. But it does happen. Someone you have been thinking about phones you out of the blue. A contact or resource you need pops up out of nowhere. You hit all the green lights when you are running late. What if instead of random occurrences, these events were all little nods or winks from the universe that you are on exactly the right path?

You might remember a time when absolutely nothing was going your way. From a synchronicity perspective, perhaps the universe is sending you a subtle message to pause or reflect or reconsider something.

Pay attention to synchronicity when it shows up in your life. The more aware you are of it, the more you will tend to see it. Be open to the possibilities. A little synchronistic event might be providing new information or opportunities to you. Be alert for clusters of events that are pointing in a particular direction.

Ultimately, you have to decide how important any synchronistic events are and attach whatever meaning to them. Just the awareness and reflection, even if you choose to dismiss it, might be sufficient to poke to your fire.

> Coincidence is God's way of
> remaining anonymous.
> —— *Albert Einstein*

: : *Shift to unattachment.*

We like to think that we have a good shot at figuring things out in life. In some ways, we want life to be predictable. That's not usually the case. John Lennon said it most beautifully: "Life is what happens while you are making other plans."

You can get stuck when things are not working out the way you had imagined. Thinking that you know for the certain the "right way" or the "right outcome" can stop you dead in your tracks when it turns out otherwise. Become unattached to the outcome of things. Let it go and trust that, even when we can't quite figure it out, everything unfolds in the way it is meant to. That concept requires a huge leap of faith. It's more challenging for people who don't believe in some greater plan for us and the world.

Consider the idea that everything that happens is a gift. Granted you might think, " I didn't really want a blender," or "What the heck is that?" But if you begin looking for the silver lining in things, you'll be surprised at what you might find. Illness might bring an opportunity to refocus on your priorities. Tough times might allow you to learn about your hidden talents and strengths. Failing to achieve a goal might help you travel down a completely new path.

Yes, there are things that happen in life that challenge our ability to find the lesson because they seem too tragic, too incomprehensible, too devastating. But those events hold the greatest growth for us.

Most of the time we are attached to things that are not nearly so significant. Look for opportunities to detach yourself from expectations and outcomes and then go with the flow. Ask yourself:

*What is there for me to learn here?*

Faith is taking the first step
even when you don't see
the whole staircase.
——— *Martin Luther King, Jr.*

## Now what?

*Are you ready to spontaneously combust?*

*Have you decided that you will no longer put your life on hold?*

*Or are you still waiting to make up your mind?*

Waiting to decide is the worst kind of waiting of all. Sometimes it's amazing what we are willing to put up with before we actually take the plunge. That's been true for me. There's great snorkeling in Bahia Santa Maria near San Jose,

Mexico. But in February the water in that cove is particularly frigid, especially if you're not wearing a wetsuit. Some of the people on our boat got right back out of the water as soon as they had gotten in. When I first climbed down the ladder I had an immediate gasp—the water was almost "take your breath away" cold. My initial reaction was "Yikes!" But knowing I wouldn't likely be back to this spot any time soon, I really wanted to check out the underwater sights. So I waited... and debated... and waited some more. After a full five minutes treading water deciding if I would get back on the boat or swim out to the reef, I had a beautiful moment of clarity: Now what? There I was stuck in limbo between the warmth of the boat and the adventure of the snorkeling. Equally good options in this case. But I was choosing to wait to decide. With every minute I was getting colder and no closer to either option. "Now what?" became a moment of spontaneous combustion. I decided to snorkel. Of course once I started swimming I warmed up a lot. It was still pretty nippy but not nearly as cold as waiting to decide.

*What are you waiting for?*

*Are you still waiting to decide?*

Don't let this be another book that just sits on your shelf. Instead let it be your call to action—your spark to set your life on fire. You can create the red hot life that you long for. You can have more.

More contribution, fulfillment, happiness.

More adventure, laughter, peace.

More of whatever you are seeking.

All you have to do is decide.

And then just begin.

Today.

## RESOURCES

Free the Children
Children helping children through education
www.freethechildren.com

Leaders Today
We are the generation we have been waiting for!
www.leaderstoday.com

Kiva
Loans that change lives
www.kiva.org

## FOR MORE INFORMATION

Please visit www.stonecirclecoaching.com

For free life coaching tips and inspiration, subscribe to Laurel's ezine *Inside the Circle* at www.stonecirclecoaching.com

Join the conversation on Laurel's blog: www.lovingchaos.com

Share your Spontaneous Combustion stories by emailing Laurel at onfire@stonecirclecoaching.com

## ABOUT THE AUTHOR

Laurel Vespi is a certified
life coach, author and
motivational speaker.
As the chief executive
guru of stone circle
coaching, she ignites
individuals, businesses and organizations to new levels
of change. Laurel relies on practical and sometimes
unconventional strategies to support people on their life
journeys, helping them get unstuck and excited.  With
humour, personal insight and story, Laurel guides people
to fresh perspectives and an awakened heart and mind.